ZEOLA, A WOMAN OF NOBLE CHARACTER

Zeola was…

> **Z**ealous for God
> **E**ager to encourage
> **O**ptimistic in her outlook
> **L**oyal in character, and
> **A**ttentive in attitude

Remembering Zeola

A Foundation Of Faith Yields A Woman Of Noble Character

BARBARA NORRIS ARYA

Library of Congress Control Number: 2024916468

ISBN
978-1-964982-34-2 (Paperback)
978-1-964982-35-9 (eBook)

TABLE OF CONTENTS

ACKNOWLEDGEMENTS

First, I thank God for giving me a loving mother who set a pattern of life and faith before me. She planted the seed for this book when she said to me a few times that I should write a book. She also began writing her own but never got back to finish it. Today her seed has come to maturity in the finished work of this book.

I thank my very capable friend who has the gift of writing as well as the technical skills in the use of the English language to read my words and discern my thoughts as she improved and clarified them in the text. Thank you, Isabella Scavetta, for using your special gifts to help me tell my stories.

Next, I want to thank my friends who were willing to read my stories in the raw and offer ways to clarify and enhance the telling of the stories. They offered many suggestions for the organization of the manuscript before Isabella was brought to it for editing. Thank you, Donna Griffith, Mary Chennette, Sue Harr, Julie Kellam and Tina Bradford. Lindy Hall took extra time because she wanted to offer suggestions only when she read it thoroughly after the first reading. Her ideas helped me to see Mom's character traits clearly.

Smitha Govindan, thank you for reading the manuscript and for drawing a diagram of the water gap. It was very helpful as it enabled me to visualize it in my mind.

Thank you, Anish, for your technical help on the computer which was very timely in putting my picture file together. Carla Schultes, thanks for help in navigating some difficulties on the Microsoft word software.

To my dear sister, Betty, whose vision was in sync with mine from the very beginning of this project. Without your help, I would not have known about Mom's manuscript. Your loving hands have been as valuable to me as if you wrote parts of the book for me. You are the reason I came to know that Mom wrote a news column since 1973 and into the year 2011 when she became wheelchair bound. You got a copy of that first article for me. We are a team in this project, and I owe you a great debt of thanks.

And finally, to my dear husband, Rakesh for computer help and to my only son, Ravi for help whenever I was able to get your attention long enough to sit down at the computer to solve a problem or to find something. Thanks to both of you for help on this project.

Part 1
Memories
From Childhood

INTRODUCTION
A STORY TO TELL

*I*n August 2004, my younger sister, Brenda, wanted to celebrate our mother's 80th birthday. Even though Brenda was in her third year of cancer treatments at the time, she was inspired to celebrate our mother, Zeola Logan Norris. She asked all seven of her sisters to help with the celebration. I was the only one who did not live in Mississippi at the time. So, I began thinking about how I could contribute to the celebration of Mom's life.

After weeks of prayerful consideration, God gave me the idea to write about Mom's life, especially of the things she loved and the things to which she had devoted her life, along with some of the struggles she had faced. As a child, growing up on the prairies of Newton County, Mississippi, Zeola learned the value of kindness, respect and love of family from her nurturing parents. As a young wife, she watched her husband go off to war just twenty- eight days after giving birth to her first child. As a mature woman, she faced the loss of her oldest son and later the loss of a daughter. Zeola's character was formed through hard work, challenges and disappointments that touched her and her family.

More importantly, Zeola's character was formed by her faith which gave her the ability to be long suffering in the trials and adversities of life. Although her trials in life were many, so too were her joys. Her life was filled with music. As soon as she got up and started her day, Zeola turned on the radio, filling the house with music. And her life was filled with celebrations for which she prepared amazing foods. She took pride in collecting special ingredients for the family celebrations. She turned butter, coconut, vanilla extract, pecans, cake flour, confectioners' sugar and eggs into delicious cakes and pies for Thanksgiving, Christmas, Easter and Revival.

Mom died in May 2013 at the age of 88. As my sister Betty cleaned out drawers and bookshelves in Mom's room, she came across a file folder in which Mom had kept obituaries and programs from various occasions. Betty found a legal pad containing the manuscript of stories that Mom had written. The pages were yellowed and wrinkled at the bottom which Mom had written perhaps thirty years earlier.

When Betty called to tell me about the manuscript, we both marveled and laughed out loud. Mom had told me a few times in the past that I should write a book. She seemed to think that I had a story to tell. Betty remembered hearing mother say, "I'm gonna write me a book!"

Was Mom thinking about this manuscript? We both wondered if her comments were her indirect way of telling us that she was actually in the process of writing at the time.

Betty sent the pages to me by mail so that I could do whatever I thought should be done to preserve the stories. When I got the package, I sat down right away to read it. Some lines had been marked out and written over as Mom made corrections which made some parts hard to read. They were stories of her childhood up till the time she was perhaps nine or ten. As I got to the end of the manuscript, I was disappointed that she had written nothing about her faith. Her book was incomplete. Somehow, she never had gotten back to write more.

What follows is Zeola's story as she remembered it and as I remember it. As always, Mom was right: I do have a story to tell, and it is her story which is now our story.

CHAPTER 1

STORIES TOLD IN ZEOLA'S WORDS

Born Into a Blended Family, a short Biography by Barbara

Zeola was born to George Noble and Ada Davis Logan on August 20, 1924, on a farm in a rural community in the prairies near Newton, Mississippi. Papa George, Zeola's father, was a widow with two small children to raise, when he met and married Ada Davis. Zeola, my mother, was the fourth of five sisters, and the eighth child of Papa George. After Zeola's birth, Mama Ada gave birth to six more children: another girl and five more boys. So, Zeola became one of fourteen children blended into one big family.

Zeola was five years old when the stock market crashed in October 1929. Her family survived the market crash since they had no money invested in the market. The farm supplied them with plenty of food throughout the Great Depression. However, they experienced a shortage of money which made it difficult to buy pantry supplies, such as flour, sugar, salt, baking powder and soda which were used daily in cooking. The farm also supplied the wood they needed for fuel. The stove for cooking burned wood all year long. In winter, the house was heated by a fireplace which burned wood. Cutting and hauling wood in a wagon was an unending chore. At night, the house was lit by oil lamps. In recalling her childhood, Zeola wrote: "Our home was shabby, but we loved it; we were happy. We played games in the yard with each other."

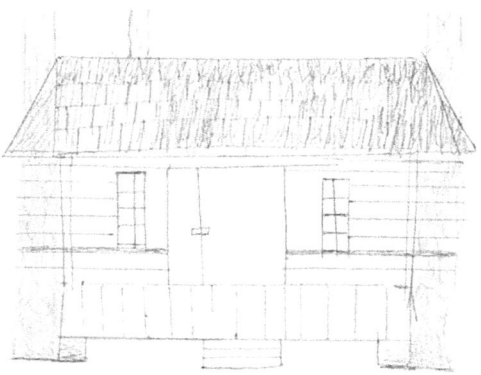

Mom's drawing of the Family Home

Mom's Self Portrait

Memories of My Physical Appearance

I had nice smooth brown skin and a big head of long, tangled hair. My braids had big, "nappy balls" on the end. My sisters all said it was hard to comb. My older sister Eliza would wash, comb and straighten my hair with a hot iron. Another big sister, Precious, would comb my sister Alla's1 hair. It took longer to do my hair because it was so thick and long.

I remember grinning and making ugly faces at my older sisters when they told me to do something. I would put my fingers in my mouth and put my index fingers in the corner my mouth, then pull my eye lids at the bottom and make it look awful. I would make loud noises so I wouldn't hear what they said as I ran fast toward them. I did that a long time. My older sisters called me "Wild Emma," because I acted wild. I did that so much that I stretched my mouth bigger than it should have been.

Even though I acted wild, I was the runt of the family, often sick with fever, or covered with sores. I was sick with malaria once in my childhood. Mosquitoes or bed bugs bit us at night. I must have been their favorite meal because I got the most bites. The bites on my legs were a big problem in the morning while we did outside chores. The dew made our legs wet. Some days or weeks later, sores began to form on my legs. Some of the sores stayed on my legs most of the year. Alla didn't get sores like I did, so she could go outside while I had to stay inside. Mama or Papa would put salve on the sores, but they stayed almost year-round.

At times, we could see the "wiggle tails" (young mosquitoes) in the drinking water. I guess the water was bad for me since I was the only one who got sick. But when I was well, I was happy and acting wild. I'll never forget the time I was sick and in bed a few days. Papa knew I was really sick, so he went to get medicine from Dr. Sharron, a lady doctor in Lake, Mississippi. I remember Papa came into the room with a big bottle of medicine in his hand. He gave me a spoonful of the medicine then stayed in the room with me all the morning, looking at me often as he read and prayed over me. Papa read a lot, and that morning he never left the room. I must have been very sick because he kept giving me medicine. I got better rather quickly because Papa doctored on me all that day. A few days later I remember getting up and doing things as usual. I think I was nine years old. I don't remember getting sick anymore. I was out with Alla from then on. We did our chores together, whatever Mama told us to do to help with housework.

Life on the Farm

I grew up on a farm in a big, poor family. During school times we went off to school very early. All of us walked through the woods to get to school each day. We walked a lot. We walked long distances to buy groceries. We faced many disadvantages, but we always had plenty of food: milk, butter, fresh vegetables, eggs, chickens, turkeys, and hogs for meat. These early years included the depression years and the years following the stock market crash in 1929. At that time, our brother Otis was a big boy and the oldest of us. He did whatever Papa did. I remember Papa, Otis, Judie, Precious and Eliza would get up before day every morning and milk cows. They strained the milk right away, then poured it into a galvanized milk can. Papa or Otis would take the big can of fresh milk to the milk truck that carried all the milk to Newton to sell. Papa used the money to provide for his family. They always kept milk for our drinking too. They strained our milk and put it away at home. We were never without milk, eggs and butter.

As we got older, Papa taught Alla and me to milk those little cows that had calves. Every evening we would get a small bucket and go from cow to cow, milking the little cows. At the same time, the young calves were having trouble with their navels. Papa looked to see what was happening to the calves' navels. He found worms in their navels. So he took some turpentine and had us hold their legs while he poured it into their navels. It seemed that the worms would get close together and close the hole, so the turpentine couldn't harm them. Papa went to town to inquire about the matter. He learned that these were "screw worms" and was given a salve to use on them. The salve did the trick and all of the calves got well.

Earliest Memories

The earliest memories I have of my childhood are when I was around four years old. I remember one day I got out of the bed where my sister Alla and I slept. Our bed was in the same room where Mama and Papa slept. Both of them were up, and our baby brother George, who slept with Mama and Papa, was not in the bed. My sister Alla was out of bed too. I remember getting up, looking in the bed for little George. The bed was soiled from his dirty diaper; a yellow stain was left. It looked bad to me. I vaguely remember getting water and soap in the wash pan; then I cleaned the soiled bed. I remember feeling good when I got it pretty clean so that it looked better to me. When Mama saw that the bed was clean, she was happy. That was the beginning of me wanting to keep things clean.

Another memory of my growing up and cleaning has to do with the cotton mattresses we slept on and which Mama made. Often, we would "unpen" a mattress so as to make it level. I remember stretching my arms long to stir the cotton inside the mattress until the mattress looked level to me. Then I would pen it back and put sheets on the bed. I put pillowcases on the pillows and made the bed really pretty. On Sundays, I would put pretty sheets on the beds for bedspreads.

It seems like I was the one that wanted things pretty all the time. After I finished the beds, I swept the floors with one of the straw2 brooms that we made. Mama taught Alla and me to wash, rinse and dry the dishes and put them away in the safe which is a metal cabinet where dishes and other serving items were stored. I would clean the dinner table and wash the dishes. I would put a white tablecloth on the table and a clean quart jar half full of water. Then I would go out and gather some flowers. I took the flowers inside, put them in the jar, and set the bouquet in the middle of the table. It looked so pretty to me with the pretty flower blooms on the white cloth. I really loved to make the house look pretty. I kept that habit as I grew up.

Memories of Daily Chores

Our morning chores were many. We had to draw water out of the well and take it into the house. Keeping enough water for cooking and drinking was a very big job. The bucket was tied to a rope which we had to pull up out of the well. We filled big buckets of water then carried them inside. Alla and I dreaded this job because the buckets were heavy. We might as well have liked it because we had to do it anyway. We had to go and draw water, bucket after bucket, as often as it ran out. In addition to keeping water for the house, Alla and I had to keep water in the trough outside for our chickens and dogs. All of these were morning chores we did every day, especially during farming season.

Our well was about four or five feet square; it held water year round. Our well never went dry although it would get low enough that we could see the bottom. It was only for household use especially drinking, washing dishes and cooking. We could see down into the well. The water was clear all the time. The well was covered with planks to protect it from animal pollution. A long V- shaped gutter was nailed to the edge of the roof of the house. The water ran from the roof into the well. So, if it rained, the water increased in the well. If it didn't rain for a long period of time, Papa and Mama would have water to use even if water was low in the well.

Papa and Otis (my oldest brother at the time) hauled water in large drums which we kept on hand for that purpose. All of our neighbors kept such drums. So, when the water in the well was getting low, we used water from the drums for watering the chickens, pigs, hogs, dogs, and other animals. The cows and livestock drank from the streams nearby and from the pond in the pasture if it had water. Papa had a pond dug, not so big, but the stagnant water dried up during the dry periods.

After we brought in water, a pot of it was heated which we used to wash dishes. Mama made the soap we used from ashes, lard and lye, a very strong chemical used in soap making. She called it "lye soap." It had a clean scent and when we washed the dishes, they sparkled. We put the dishes away in the safe- which was a metal cabinet with shelves and drawers that held the dishes and cooking utensils.

After we finished the dishes, Mama gave us the big sink bucket. We had to go to the garden and pick butterbeans, peas, or snap beans; whichever vegetable she preferred. We loved to pick the butterbeans more than the snap beans; peas were the next preference. After picking peas or beans, the next chore was to shell (remove the hull) them for dinner. We loved shelling the colored butterbeans which had lots of pretty colors. We would try to match colors sometimes, but we had to remember to hurry because they were for dinner. Some mornings we picked strawberries and had to hurry picking, remove the stems and get them ready for Mama to cook for a dinner treat for Papa and the family. Mama spent most of her time preparing meals and tending her babies.

Mama worked hard to get the meals ready on time. Alla and I were a lot of help to her. After shelling beans or peas, we would pick up the hulls, sweep the porch, then carry the hulls and throw them away. If we had a "hair of a chance," we would play. If Mama heard us, she might give us another job. For example, she might say, "Go make the beds!" if they were not made already.

I recall many days on the farm doing many different chores. Some days Mama would send Alla and me to the field where Papa and Otis had cleared a new field. We had to pile up brush and bushes and stack them in a pile. We probably would do a half day of piling brush. After dinner Mama might let us go fishing on Uncle Alf's water gap. The water gap was big and deep. Oh what a fun time for us! We would dig earth worms, put them in a can and cover them with soil as we dug them up because they were so slimy. Keeping covered with soil helped to handle them better. Sometimes we caught nice perch; sometimes we caught a big goggle eye perch or two.

At other times we caught two or three yellow bellies, or blue gills, or maybe a catfish. Sometimes we caught a big crawdad that would put up a fight by pinching our fingers. The crawdads caught our fingers a few times and boy did that hurt! Oh how our fingers hurt! Once, a crawdad pinched Alla's index finger so badly that a red dot came in the middle of her fingernail. She cursed the crawdad and called it ugly names while she stomped it dead. I laughed about it which made her more angry, so she called me a fool.

Memories of the Water Gap

The water gap was on Uncle Braggs farm. It was built on Cedar Creek which was a small stream of water near our farm. It was built directly in the creek bed. They looked for a big tree on either side of the creek that looked promising to make a good watering hole. Once the trees were located, skidder wire (a very strong metal wire) was used to run across the creek. They put the skidder wire around each tree, real tight so it wouldn't come loose. Once the wire was secure, they put the first layer of planks across the stream very close together so that no cracks were left between them. Next, they placed the ends of other planks on the bottom of the creek so that each plank leaned forward resting on the skidder wire. They closed the cracks while reaching each side of the creek bank. Next, they took another layer of thick planks, punching the ends into the bottom of the creek and leaning them forward the same way, but on the opposite side.

This layer of planks was to cover any cracks that remained which also cut off the flow of the water. The planks would carry the water over the sag in the middle of the gap, making the water run really fast. And as the water ran, it washed out the dirt, making the hole deeper and wider, eventually making a pond that would hold water all year. The water gap seldom dried up during dry seasons but kept water available for the farmers' animals and Uncle Bragg's big beautiful horse named Dan. The water gap was worthwhile because they had water regardless of whether it rained enough during summers.

All farmers that owned stock, such as horses, mules, and cows, would go a little farther down that same creek and make their own water gaps. They, too, could have plenty of water for their livestock throughout the dry season. This was a great invention because it solved their water shortage problems.

Our Neighbors and Community

Dad's relative, Aunt Louisa, lived a short distance down the road from our house3. She was old, but pretty, and wore her hair in four long black braids. She didn't have her own cistern, so she got water from our cistern. She had nobody to help her carry water for cooking and drinking. So, she carried the full bucket on her head. Because she lived alone, she didn't need a lot of water. She was a dear neighbor. She had a granddaughter whose name was Amanda Bender who was my playmate whenever she came for a visit.

Aunt Louisa's yards were sandy which made it easy to sweep them with a straw broom. Her flowers grew around the fence on the front while the back yard had pecan and pear trees growing. Mama would borrow a little soda, or salt from her sometimes and also shared vegetables, milk, and other foods which Aunt Louisa didn't have. Aunt Louisa's sister, Kate Bender lived with Uncle Alf, their brother. Mama would let me spend the night with Kate and Uncle Alf. Both of them were clean; their houses and yards were kept well. Uncle Alf's hog pen and a big chicken yard were kept very clean.

Mama would send us over to Robert's grocery store if she needed some groceries. We walked behind our house, crawled under Papa's fence, then under Mr. Floyd Gordy's fence to cut off some of the distance. Whenever we passed Mr. Gordy's house, the dogs charged at us which made us afraid. Alla always ran, yelling, cursing and crying. Thank God the dogs ran passed me. When they stopped chasing Alla, they went back home. We were both afraid, but they didn't bother me, so I was happy. I guess they got tired of chasing Alla since she gave them a "run for the money." As we continued our long walk back home, we had to crawl under another fence, cross Mr. Gordy's pasture again and hope we wouldn't see his dogs or cows. The cows were another dread.

Sometimes we ran up the hill to Mr. Everett's store. Alla gave the bill to the storekeeper who put the items in a sack. Sometimes Mama had too many things on the bill. A few times, Alla would carry a 25-pound sack of flour and I would carry the meal, sugar and other items in a cloth sack. By the time we passed Mr. Floyd Gordy's house with the groceries, if the dogs barked, someone in the house would make them go away. Alla and I were spared a run with the groceries. Mama was very glad to see us coming back so she could finish dinner. After such a trip, Mama would let us take a rest which we welcomed.

Part 2
Zeola's Life Told
By Barbara

CHAPTER 2

MARRIAGE AND THE WAR YEARS

*B*y 1940, Zeola was a 16-year-old who loved to go with her Dad to many different churches where he taught how to read and sing the shaped notes, also called solmization. (Solmization is a system of attributing a distinct syllable to each note in a musical scale: do, re, mi, fa, sol, la, ti, do.) On one such trip, she met John Wiley (JW) Norris, Jr. down in the hills of Smith County, Raleigh, Mississippi. JW was the son of John Wiley, Sr. and Georgia Lyles Norris. According to Mom, because JW was the youngest of ten children, his mother cherished and spoiled him greatly. He had attended the Norris School which his father had helped organize and was taught by his father and two older sisters. But he went to school for only five years before leaving school to work. He was about fifteen years old at the time he left school.

As Zeola and JW got to know each other, JW asked her to marry him. With the approval of her parents, Zeola and JW were married in August 1940. Zeola was just sixteen. JW took her into his parents' home while he spent his days helping his older brothers cut pulp wood and logs and hauled them to a mill for sale. To Mom's benefit, there were others in the household to talk with and do chores with. Because Zeola was only sixteen, she willingly did whatever they asked or told her to do. She helped her mother- and sisters-in- law cook, clean, wash dishes and do all of the chores that needed to be done. She didn't assert herself nor focus on her rights but worked to complete the tasks to be done.

On January 1, 1943, Zeola gave birth to her first child: a son who was named Aaron Percy. Mom told us that her sisters-in-law chose the name "Aaron Percy" for their two older brothers—Aaron and Percy. Both brothers were drafted into the army, and both left for World War II on December 8, 1942. A few short weeks after Aaron's birth, JW had to report for enlistment in January 1943, even though his son was only four weeks old. I wonder if Dad had a choice to accept or decline enlistment, but he went on because he knew his parents would make sure Mom and baby Aaron were taken care of.

Dad shared details of his military service with me in the last few years of his life. He was able to recall some details in 2010 when we celebrated his 90th birthday. Other stories I record here were told to us by Dad and Mom during our childhood.

JW reported to Camp Shelby, near Hattiesburg, Mississippi, on January 28, 1943, for initiation into the military. From Camp Shelby, his company was soon transported to the Aberdeen Proving Grounds, which was a major army training post in Maryland during World War II. After going through some procedures and training for perhaps six months, his company was transported to Fort Drum Army Base, in New York.

After a time at Fort Drum, Dad's company was put on a ship that set sail for Australia, New Guinea and the Philippines. He recalled how they attempted to communicate with the natives they met along the way. He didn't recall the year his ship reached the Philippines, but he did remember that when he reached there his company was under the command of General McArthur. General MacArthur was assigned to command all of the forces in the Philippines in 1944, with the purpose of defeating the Japanese in the Philippines. Once in the Philippines, Dad's company began the hard work of cutting trees and making roads and air strips through the jungle for military vehicles and equipment. Dad spoke about the times when they had to jump off the machines and run into foxholes for safety. He survived the gunfire and the "jungle fever" he contracted. His discharge papers show that he was hospitalized for a time. He recalled that he had a severe rash and could not wear his shoes. He got it on his hands as well. Thankfully, the rash went away after treatment. Dad also told how he met his oldest brother, Aaron, somewhere in the Pacific before Aaron returned home to the United States in December 1944. They delighted to remember how and where they met and how it was a heartwarming surprise for both brothers.

In August 1945, the Japanese forces were quickly advancing toward another victory, so pressure was increased to stop their progress. Dad remembered when the soldiers got word that the atomic bomb had stunned the Japanese forces, but the Emperor was so determined to win the battle that he ignored the devastation of the city of Hiroshima. Because of that decision, a second bomb was dropped on Nagasaki a few days later. Shortly thereafter, the Emperor called for an end to the war.

Suddenly, the war was over. Dad had been spared the worst of the battles in the Luzon area. He didn't remember whether it took a few weeks or months before his company was back in the states. His discharge papers note that he was back in the United States and honorably discharged on November 29, 1945.

With the war over, Dad found himself back home in Mississippi with his wife and two-year-old son. Unlike his brother Aaron who had suffered a gunshot wound to his neck, Dad had been spared the terrors of the war and returned home without any visible scars of World War II. I can imagine how Zeola's anxiety was suddenly turned into joy. Her sadness and long-suffering were replaced by great gladness for herself and the family. Both of Dad's parents were alive when their beloved sons returned home alive from the war.

A Home for JW and Zeola's Family

Once JW was home, he began planning to build a house for his family. JW's father had saved the money he had earned while he was in the service for two years. JW used that money to buy lumber to build their house. He got his Uncle Fela, his dad's youngest brother, to guide the building of the house. Uncle Fela knew some of the basics of how to construct a house and had some tools. According to Joyce, Uncle Fela's youngest child, Uncle Fela learned the construction skills when he was a student in the late 1930's at Prentiss Institute, in Prentiss, Mississippi.

Together, the two men built a simple 'shot-gun' house with six rooms. Four rooms were bedrooms, and two others were the kitchen and dining room. The house was left in its natural state. We could see the beams, nails, and splinters in the wood where nails went askew. And the walls lacked smoothness and paint. Consequently, we often got pricks and scratches or splinters in the flesh if we got too close to the walls. Sometimes, we tore our clothes on the walls. We learned to be very careful about getting too close to the walls. The house lacked a bathroom with a toilet, tub and sink in it. The kitchen didn't have cabinets and counter tops. Nor did it have fixtures, such as a sink to wash dishes. A bucket was kept in the kitchen for throw away food to be fed to the animals daily. Dishwater was thrown out the door along with foods that spoiled.

Yet, this house gave Zeola a home of her own and some sweet relief from the demands her sisters-in-law made upon her. Eight of Zeola's children were born in this six-room house. For many years, the walls withstood the wind and rain. The windows stayed in place and the roof stayed on. Also, the chimney sent the smoke outside, while the wood-burning fireplace kept us warm through the winters.

Chapter 3

Childbearing
Years Resume

*I*n August of 1946, Zeola gave birth to her second child, Betty. That winter was a very rough one as many children in the community got pneumonia and a few of them died.

When she was only a few months old, Betty got very ill and the parents thought they would lose her to pneumonia. JW loved to tell how he sought medical help from his mother and his elderly aunt who went to the house and did all they knew to help make his little baby well. The only medicines at hand were camphor, cod liver oil, and asafetida, which they used along with many prayers. The ingredients were made into a kind of salve. They anointed her body, kept her warm, and stayed beside the fire. By the grace of God, Betty recovered and was healthy after that scare. Zeola once again learned how to pray as she saw God answer her prayers.

About fourteen months later, in 1947, Zeola gave birth to a second girl. Grandma Georgia wanted to name her "Rachael Eudora," but her sisters-in-law objected strongly. They didn't want their nieces to be named after any of Grandma's sisters.

So, they filled out the information for birth registration and wrote my name as Barbara Josephine. The crisis Zeola faced with me did not occur in my infancy. I was around four years old when I got sores all over my head, which may have been caused by chicken pox or ringworms. My head was so covered with sores that Mom had to cut off all of my hair in order to treat them and make me well.

Gloria, who is next to me in age, was born fifteen months later. Gloria grew to be a glib talker with a quick sense of humor. She made us laugh many times as she expressed in her own unique way what she observed. She used her quick wit on many people who often didn't get her drift until others were laughing. Dad's father called her "mule train" because she danced whenever she heard the song on the radio. Her quick wit and the way she imitated others made the family laugh. Next in the birth order was another girl, who was named Brenda. She arrived on December 1, 1951. Most of the family called her "Bren or Faye," but one of Dad's brothers called her "Blendie Faye," which always made us laugh. She had a keen eye and knew where Mom hid things, she didn't want us to find. When Mom could not find something, Faye would get it and bring it to her.

We were mystified by this knowledge which Faye had. Faye also had a keen intellect.

Zeola gave birth to a fifth girl on July 4th of 1953. Sybil arrived on a holiday, but for Mom, new baby and the other children, it was just another day. Mom chose the name Sybil after she found the name in a story she read. A second son, Dell, was born to the family on February 22, 1955. The year after Dell was born, Zeola experienced her first big accident with one of her babies. She had a pot of hot water setting on the fireplace hearth because she was going to use it. But, before she had a chance, Dell, the toddler got to it and turned it over on himself. Mom had a difficult time taking off the hot clothes from his body because the water was very hot. Dell's burns were primarily on his bottom and his legs and perhaps a hand and fingers. His face was spared. This painful time lasted for weeks if not months, quieting him and taking care of the burns. I was perhaps eight years old at the time. Somehow, Dell's burns healed, and life continued on for Zeola and her seven children.

A few years later, Zeola had a second "threat of disaster" with her young son who was probably four years old at the time. On a certain day after we had eaten dinner, Mom threatened to whip Dell for doing something she told him not to do. He must have continued doing it, so she got up to stop him, but Dell ran out the door. Mom ran after him but he outran her. She called us to catch him, but Dell outran us too and headed across the road and into the pasture toward the pond. None of us could swim, so we all became very frightened as Dell ran closer to the pond. Tension was suddenly very high. What were we going to do? Truly, Dell's guardian angel was watching out for him. God saw our plight and sent "help from heaven." Our cousin, James Walter, who was a teenager at the time, came riding up on his horse. He saw what was about to happen, so he quickly got off the horse and ran to Dell. Even though Dell ran into the pond, he didn't get far before James caught him and picked him up. Our hearts recovered from that ordeal. Mom must have praised God mightily for His providential care that day which saved her young son's life.

In February 1957, Mom gave birth to twin girls. She told us that Dr. Coursey, the family doctor, named them Mary and Martha. Mom sometimes commented that Dr. Coursey had an uncanny accuracy in assigning their names. Each of the names was apt for their personality and temperament. Mary was the gentle natured one who looked out for her little sister. Martha was the one who fought for what she wanted, often taking whatever, she wanted from Mary who hardly ever cried. We wanted Mary to stand up to Martha, but she wouldn't. She gave in to Martha's demands and seldom made a fuss to have her way. The twins brought the number of children to nine; seven of which were girls.

Mom got a break from childbearing for nine years. Dad told us that he was teased by his peers about having so many girls. But Dad worked us as if we were boys.

Daily Chores and Learning Responsibility

The family continued to live in the "shotgun" house. As with her mother before her, Zeola's days were filled with caring for her babies, preparing three meals each day, and training the oldest children to help with daily chores while the younger ones watched and tended the babies. Our daily chores included washing the dishes, sweeping the floors, taking out trash, and other jobs as they came up. We had to sweep the floors at least once a day and take out the chamber pot (a bed pan) each morning to dump out the waste and rinse out the pan before bringing it back into the house.

All of us had to bring in wood and make fires in the stove to cook and in the fireplace to heat the house in winter. The older girls helped by drawing water from the well and bringing it into the house many times across the day. We learned to make the covers straight on the beds and put away dirty clothes until wash day. Betty, the oldest girl, was eleven and was learning to help by combing her sisters' hair. Betty was adept at helping Mom to assign tasks to be done. She had big, round eyes that were often on the lookout for jobs to be done. She specialized in finding the most dreaded task to be done; then she would go to Mom and tell her to have me do it. She would begin by making it clear that she was already working on some other task, and that is why I must do it. Mom seemed to go along with Betty's suggestions which made me very angry. This was one thing I hated about Betty and it caused Mom to think badly of me. Mom said I was stubborn and that I worked against Betty in such jobs whenever she had both of us doing a task together. Other than that, Betty and I were best friends and buddies.

No matter the time of year, we had evening chores to do before night. If we forgot to do a job, for example take the chamber pot inside, Mom made us go out in the dark to get it. That was very scary for whoever had to go. Usually, two of us would go out together if it were already night. We had to get water in for the night as well. If there were cows and calves to put into the barn, we had to do that early in the evening as well.

Our clothes were gathered daily from the bedrooms and put aside until wash day. Once a week, the clothes were all taken to the pond across the road from the house. At the pond, water was plentiful to wash and rinse everything. We filled a tub with water; then we rubbed the clothes on a washboard using soap Mom made. After washing, we rinsed the clothes in clean water before we took them back to the house where we hung them out on the fence to dry. This job was very hard work, but Mom supervised it all.

The birth of the twins prompted Dad to buy a washing machine. It relieved us from hauling so many clothes to the pond and back. We delighted very much in the new washer which also had a wringer in it. We had to put the clothes into the tub of rinse water; then feed them through the wringer to get most of the water out. A family joke even to this day is told about me getting my arm caught in the wringer with the clothes. The joke Gloria and Betty tell is that they would look up and see me coming through the wringer; not just my hand or arm, but all of me. I did get my arm or hand caught a few times until Mom decided that I was not skilled enough to manage the wringer. So, I didn't have to do that job but, still had to help hang the clothes out to dry on the lines in the yard. After the clothes dried, we had to take them off the line and carry them into the house.

Speed Queen Wringer Washing Machine

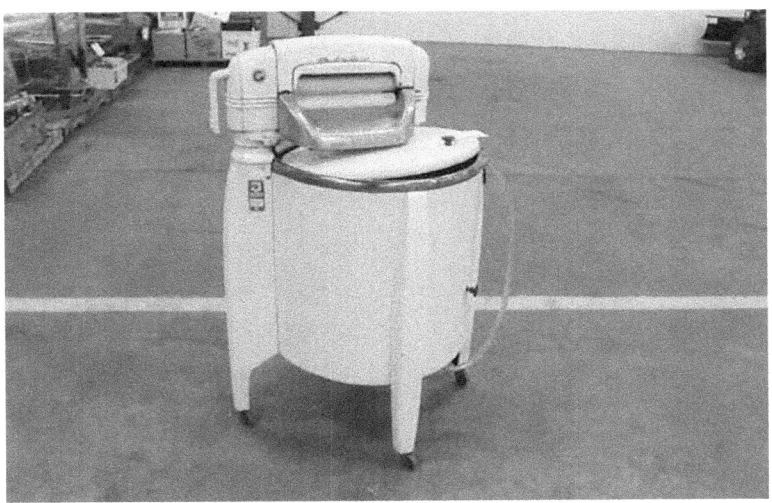

Wash day was not over until all the clothes were folded and put away. Sometimes, clothes had to be pressed with the hot iron which was heated on the coals in the fireplace. That job was very dangerous. Sometimes we got burned by the iron because it was very hot. So we learned how to be very careful when we ironed. By the time summer arrived, we could play outside more often. A favorite activity was to create a playhouse. We pretended we had babies that we put in a play bed. We pretended to cook food and eat in our playhouse. This provided us relief from our chores and was a shared delight.

CHAPTER 4

SHE DARED TO DISCIPLINE

*M*om was proud of all her children. She was very diligent to correct us firmly and with the rod whenever we disobeyed certain rules. Zeola was determined that she would not spoil any of her children. She recited many verses of scripture in her teaching and correcting us. A favorite verse she quoted was Proverbs 13:24, which she abbreviated to say, "Spare the rod and spoil the child." The complete verse says: He who spares the rod hates his son, but he who loves him is careful to discipline him. Another Proverb she applied in this matter says: Discipline your son while there is hope. If you beat him with a rod, he will not die. Beat him with a rod and deliver his soul from hell. (23;13-14.)

She quoted many times Proverbs 22:15: Foolishness is bound up in the heart of a child; the rod of correction will drive it far from him. So, the "switch" was Zeola's favorite tool of correction which she made us go out to get. We broke a small branch from a bush, stripped the leaves from it, and then took it to her. That was a dreaded event because we knew we would get no "mercy." We learned quickly to control our anger and crying.

She gave us a little time to dry the face and to never stomp away from her after a correction. That was how she reinforced her words of correction. We were wise to heed her words, or we paid the penalty.

Learning to Sew

Singer Treadle Sewing Machine

After the birth of Sybil, with five small girls all needing things to wear, Mom learned how to be creative and to sew clothes for her girls especially. Mama Georgia owned a sewing machine which Zeola learned to operate. It was a "treadle" machine powered with a foot pedal. When her oldest sister, Tot moved nearby with her own machine, Zeola began to learn many more things about sewing. Once she learned how to use the machine, her sister helped her make dresses and little coats for winter, and to remake things for us out of fabric that had been some other item of clothing. When flour began to come in 25lb sacks, soon we had dresses made from flour sacks. Some of the sacks were quite pretty which meant we would get a pretty, colorful dress.

Later on, as we grew older, Mom began to teach me to sew. She taught me to use the foot pedal. She also taught me how to sew a straight seam by using the base of the sewing pad to guide me. And she taught me how to thread the machine which involved a few steps. Once I could sew without Mom standing over me, she used me to sew many things, such as hems that had to be adjusted, then skirts and later on dresses for us. Other items included sewing pockets, zippers, Ric Rac and lace on dresses. Making buttonholes came much later when Mom bought a buttonhole attachment. She was there to guide me whenever I got into a difficult spot. Sometimes, she had to pick out a seam and sew it herself.

Zeola learned many things from her sister who had become a seamstress and bought her own sewing machine. When Auntie's family broke apart and she moved away, she gave Zeola her machine. Through trial and error, she learned how to repair it and clean out the lint from the internal parts as well. For example, when the bobbin mis-threaded and stitches didn't tie correctly, she learned what was needed and she fixed it. She learned the importance of oil and where and how to oil the parts that needed oil for maximum performance. She was very quick to learn and a good reader. These skills helped her to learn how to read patterns and to cut and follow the directions to make new dresses, skirts and blouses for her daughters and for herself. She even made my senior prom dress a few years later.

Mom made me a beautiful pink dress with a long waist and small pleats all around the bottom. I didn't have a date for the prom, but Mom went with me. I knew my dress was pretty and that is the best memory I have of the prom. The last and biggest project that Mom and I did was to make choir robes for our church choir. I was home from college after my second year when the decision was made to make robes for the choir. Mom did all of the cutting of perhaps twenty- five robes out of cotton fabric. I did the sewing until I got a problem that she had to correct. And the money we were paid for all of that labor was $20. I vaguely remember the discussion about how much to pay us for the job. Anyway, it is all washed away in the sea of forgetfulness.

For the Love of Music

Zeola's love of music was rooted deep in her childhood. Her father, Papa George, was a good singer who traveled around to nearby African American communities teaching church groups how to read and sing the shape notes. As a girl growing up, her heart was warmed by her father's teaching. Hearing people talking about her father's wonderful voice and his skill as a teacher inspired great admiration for her father. Through her father's work, Zeola also got to travel to places beyond her community and church. Together, they went to singing conventions, such as the Solomon Union Singing Convention, where many people gathered with their song books to sing the shape notes. It was at such a gathering that Zeola met JW, her future husband.

Not only were the members of the church groups learning how to use their voices, but they were also learning to read. Many of the songs included words from the scriptures. Singing the songs helped the singers to retain the words which eventually got written onto their tongues and into their hearts. Young Zeola was learning what the adults were learning: how to use the voice, read the shape notes, read the words, memorize scriptures and recite verses of songs.

She had a big alto voice, and she sang many gospel songs as recordings were played over the radio. When Betty and I were in elementary school, Zeola taught us to sing duets. Soon we were called upon to sing at church and at school. Uncle Fela called us to sing in the singing conventions where they sang the shape notes. Later on, Zeola had three more sisters sing with us. Once the twins were old enough, they became part of the Norris Sisters group. At this point, Zeola taught us to sing soprano and alto while she sang tenor which made for good harmony.

In addition to church, the radio was an important source of music in Zeola's life. As Zeola was rearing her children, she played the radio daily and listened to both gospel and secular songs. A radio station signal that came in clearly in the mornings was WDIA, from Memphis, Tennessee. We enjoyed hearing groups such as The Angelic Gospel Singers, The Clara

Ward Singers, The Caravans, The Staple Singers, The Dixie Hummingbirds, James Cleveland, Hezekiah Walker, Mahalia Jackson, Sam Cooke and the Chicago Soul Stirrers, and the Five Blind Boys of Alabama, were among the many groups we heard during that time. In the 1960's, and beyond we listened to the radio with great interest to The Temptations, The Jackson Five, Stevie Wonder, The Supremes, James Brown, Marvin Gaye and Tammy Terrell, Aretha Franklin, and many others.

Long after her daughters were grown, Zeola continued to sing with her daughters Betty, Gloria, Brenda, and Sybil. After Brenda's death, Zeola continued singing with Betty until she had to use the wheelchair in 2011. Singing and making music was treasured by Zeola throughout her life. She and Dad followed the Solomon Union Singing Convention in their region until they both became unable to travel.

JW and Zeola honored by Solomon Union Convention

For the Love of Reading

Because of Zeola's love of reading, she got books from JW's sisters who taught school. She was the one who introduced us to the joy of reading good stories. I remember the "Dick and Jane" and "Lil' Black Sambo" stories. We had a storybook with a scary story of a wolf trying to get into the house where the children were home alone. I was very scared as that story was read. I'm not sure how early we learned to read, but I remember listening to stories read to us. Soon we were able to read stories for ourselves and to share the reading of stories together. From this period in our lives, I don't remember sitting down with Mom to read stories, but Dad was gone most days all day long so she must have read to us.

Later on, as we grew up, I remember Mom reciting the poem on the months of the year. It begins, "Thirty days have April, June, September, and November..." The poem below is included because it is one, she recited to us on many occasions in her later years. It was found in 2013 by Gloria after Mom's death in her Bible with the date that she copied it from some other source.

My Old Bible   8-1-07

Though the cover is worn,
And the pages are torn,
And though places bear traces of tears,
Yet more precious than gold
Is this Book worn and old,
That can shatter and scatter my fears.

This old Book is my guide,
'Tis a friend by my side,
It will lighten and brighten my way;
And each promise I find
Soothes and gladdens the mind,
As I read it and heed it each day.

To this Book I will cling,
Of its worth I will sing,
Though great losses and crosses
    be mine;
For I cannot despair,
Though surrounded by care,
While possessing this blessing devine.

I remember Dad telling us some of his favorite stories as well. "Brer Rabbit," "The Horned Animals Party," and "Chanticleer" are three stories Dad told us as we sat by the fire on cold winter nights. Although Dad made it only through elementary school, he somehow knew the story of "Chanticleer" as it appears in the "Nun's Priest Tale" in Geoffrey Chaucer's Canterbury Tales. He must have learned it from his father and/ or sisters. A poem Dad acted out as he told it to us was "Two Little Blackbirds." We learned many poems during our elementary and high school years. We made learning competitive by seeing who could learn the longest poem. I learned "The Night before Christmas" and "Paul Revere's Ride." My younger sisters learned "The Gingham Dog and the Calico Cat." And together we learned the "Gettysburg Address," by Abraham Lincoln.

As I go back through memories of my childhood, I recall that Auntie's children taught us to say the letters of the alphabet backwards and they helped us learn many poems. In addition, we memorized Bible passages, such as Luke 2: 1-15 which we read on every Christmas program during those years. Whenever I hear Charlie Brown reciting it, I enjoy joining in. We also memorized the "Ten Commandments," the "Twenty- Third Psalm," the "Lord's Prayer," the "Beatitudes," the books of the Old and New Testaments and many other verses of scripture. We knew many Old Testament stories. Two of my favorite Bible stories were "Joseph and his Brothers" and "Daniel in the Lion's Den."

CHAPTER 5

A YEAR OF SHARED MISERY AND HOPE

*T*he late 1950s proved to be a period of great emotional highs and lows for Zeola. Her father, Papa George, got sick with lung cancer in 1955 and died in July, 1956.

The day Papa George was buried, his youngest son Caleb recalled that it was his fifteenth birthday. Seven months after her father's death, Zeola gave birth to twin girls, Mary and Martha in February, 1957. Sometime in that same year our oldest brother, Aaron was sent away to Piney Woods School, a boarding school, about forty miles from our home. A few months later, early in June 1957, Zeola's oldest sister, Aunt Precious, (Tot, her pet name) gave birth to her own set of twin girls whom she named Ramona and Renee. The birth of the twins increased Auntie's children to ten: two boys and eight girls. The oldest son was around eighteen and the younger son was around twelve. Zeola's twins increased her children to nine: two boys and seven girls.

The problem that was already in the making was that Auntie's husband, Uncle Tood, who was Dad's oldest brother, had already left the family without warning. Auntie didn't know for sure that her husband had abandoned her for the rodeo and would not return home to provide for her and their family which now included two babies. Soon after her twins were born, Auntie came to our house to inform Mom and Dad about the miserable situation she faced. She had no food and no money to buy food for the family, and the babies were sick for lack of nourishment. How would Zeola and JW help to "bear her sister's burden?"

Upon hearing of this urgent situation, Dad took Auntie to the little grocery store in Pineville, where he used his credit to buy the family some groceries. He bought the bare essentials, such as flour, sugar, salt, baking powder and soda, meal, lard, and some pork. All of these items were necessary to cook a simple meal. Because milk was not plentiful this time of year on the farm, canned milk had to be bought for both sets of twins.

Some weeks passed with the situation unresolved. No one knew what Auntie would do to provide for her children. As summer came to an end, Mom, Dad and Auntie made a decision to move her children into the house with us while Auntie would take the oldest son with her to Joliet, Illinois, to find work. So, our cousins were brought to live with us in a six- room house without a bathroom or running water. Our mother, aged 33, was left to manage and care for seventeen children, two boys and fifteen girls, in a house with few essentials and very little living space.

Five of Auntie's children were older than Betty who turned eleven, and I was almost ten. The daily need to bring water from the well for the house, especially for the kitchen, was always at hand. Zeola was busy all the time overseeing the four babies, washing their bodies and changing their diapers.

However, we helped by washing the diapers and by washing and preparing the bottles daily. All four of the babies had to be held to nurse since Zeola's twins were about six months and Auntie's twins were hardly two months old. Mom had to do a lot of holding and comforting the younger babies especially because they were sick when she got them.

One can only imagine some of the squabbles and fights that ensued daily among so many girls. The twins and the toddlers were the only ones who could not join in the contentions. The toddlers were spared the strife that the older girls engaged in since they could hardly walk or talk. Many times, daily we fought to sit in the prized chair or to drink from the best glass or eat with the shiniest spoon or on the best plate.

Zeola served the food onto our plates or else some of us wouldn't have anything to eat. She made biscuits every morning and cornbread for lunch and dinner to eat with our vegetables and a piece of meat if there was any. Many a breakfast consisted of egg gravy and biscuits, or scrambled mackerels with egg and biscuits. We grew plenty of collard greens, mustards and turnip greens, and sweet potatoes for winter. We grew sugar cane to make syrup for the winter meals. We grew peanuts which were parched and eaten for a very special treat on many winter nights. Because of the crops, there was enough food to feed seventeen children and two adults.

Auntie and her son did find work, and by November of 1957, they had earned enough money to send train tickets for the children to come live with her. Hope was revived in both sisters' hearts once Aunt Tot sent the tickets for her children. Mom cooked food, fried chicken, eggs and pork meat for biscuits, and teacakes for something sweet. She packed a bag lunch for seven children who would certainly get hungry on their long journey to Joliet, Illinois. And they even took bottles of milk for the babies who were only four months old at the time. I wonder how the older girls managed the babies and keep their milk safe to drink. Looking back now, I know that God provided for them and kept them all safe on the trip. One Saturday morning before Thanksgiving, Dad borrowed a car from his sister, Aunt Lorna; loaded the children, the bagged lunch, and a few items they could take along; then drove them to Jackson, Mississippi. They boarded the City of New Orleans train for Joliet, Illinois. Zeola must have sent many urgent prayers up to God for a safe journey for the children and especially for the babies.

On that Thanksgiving Day, I don't remember any celebration. It must have been a mixture of grief and relief for Zeola. She was anxious about the twins and concerned for their wellbeing on the long trip. But she was also relieved that she now had only two babies to care for and fewer fights to deal with. For her nine children, it was sweet relief. Having our cousins in the house had been stressful for all of us. I am thankful that the Lord kept Mom's wits about her and kept Dad strong and healthy as they both worked diligently to provide for seventeen children through the four-month ordeal. They found a way to help Auntie survive this period of turmoil. Only by God's grace did we all survive this very stressful time. Thankfully, it had come to a "hope- filled" end as Auntie was reunited with her nine children.

Uncle Tood Returns

Around 1972, Uncle Tood, Dad's brother made contact through someone to let his brothers know that he was alive and wanted to return to Mississippi. Dad followed up on the contact in New Mexico, and soon after that, he took uncle Tood first to his family in Joliet, IL which lasted only a week or two. After that, Uncle was brought to his brother, Aaron's home where he lived during the week. On weekends, JW brought him to his home, then took him back to Aaron's home on Sunday evenings. They continued to share in keeping their brother for the remainder of his days. Upon his death, Auntie, one son and five older daughters returned to his funeral in January 1976. One daughter came by the house to visit with us when Mom's sister, Aunt Alla died in November 2005.

However, none of our cousins came to Mom's or Dad's funerals in 2013 and 2014. We have not seen the other siblings since they left Mississippi 58 years ago. Five of the ten siblings are now deceased, but I hope to see the five who are still alive someday in the future.

CHAPTER 6

A MODERN FAMILY HOME

*D*ad's brother, Aaron, and his family lived in the old, Wiley Norris family home which was affectionately called "the big house." By 1959, Uncle Aaron contracted and built a house for his family. They moved into it by the end of that summer. When Uncle Aaron moved out of the old family home, Dad moved his family into it because it was his inheritance. The family home was a ten-room house which gave us more living space, but it needed many repairs and replacements. So, in 1960, Dad decided to build a new house for his family.

The prospect of our own new house was very exciting. Dad contracted with the same builder that Uncle Aaron had used. The contractor showed Mom and Dad a house plan he could build for them which would give them a kitchen, dining room, family room, living room, bathroom and three bedrooms with closets; eight rooms altogether. So, Dad signed on, and the construction process began.

Materials had to be bought; the most expensive part seemed to be the cost of the lumber needed. After learning about the cost of new lumber, Dad decided to use the lumber from the "shotgun" house along with whatever could be salvaged from the old family home to build the new house. But one problem was not addressed: Where would the family live while the old houses were taken down? Again, Dad sought the help of his Uncle Fela to build a temporary house. Together, they constructed a "tin house" that would keep the family and house contents protected while the new house was built. Once the temporary house was built, we moved into it, and the old houses were torn down. We lived in the tin house from June until early October 1960, when we moved into the new house. That was a very exciting time for the whole family.

When we saw our beautiful new home with its smooth walls, bright colors, and spacious rooms, our eyes popped, and we were ecstatic with joy at the thought of living in such a house. We finally had a bathroom with a door, and lights in the ceilings of every room as well as outlets. The rooms were painted in beautiful colors which we found exciting since we could go from a pink room into a green or a blue room. Our rooms also had closets in which we could put our clothes and shoes. The kitchen had many cabinets, smooth countertops, and smooth floors.

We had a dining room to eat in and a living room to sit in. The two rooms were separated by a very special relic from Dad's family home. He preserved the set of French doors that were a treasured item from his family home; so, he asked the builder to use them in his new home. Today, the doors remain in our house as a reminder of our heritage. I am amazed that the glass still holds together in all of the little windows. I wonder now about the quality of the glass because all of the little panes are still there in the door. We had no sofa or soft chairs to sit on at the time we moved into the house. These items would be bought years later. Plumbing would also take a few years to become a reality. It was installed in 1969, when Betty and I began teaching school, and Mom had a job with Head Start.

Photo of Modern Family Home Taken by Gloria in 2016

A Family Broken Apart

The summer of 1961 was a memorable one. People commented that it rained every day the whole month of June. I remember the daily rains. There was a weather pattern that caused extreme drought on the west coast and excessive rain on the east coast from June into July of 1961. The rain destroyed Dad's crops along with all of the neighbors' crops. We couldn't chop or hoe nor plow anything: the weeds overgrew the cotton, corn and vegetable crops.

The watermelons just kept growing, and many rotted in the field because they lay in puddles of water. Mom and Dad observed that "the melons took the second growth." The ones that appeared to be mature were not sweet, only partially ripe. The loss of the crops created great stress for all the farmers.

Mom and Dad had taken out a bank loan to buy seeds and fertilizer to plant crops for the year. Now there was no harvest to pay for the crop and house loans.

In late, August, Dad and Mom decided to leave us with Dad's oldest sister so they could go to Illinois to find work. They moved in with Mom's sister and family. Mom got work in a nursing home alongside Dad's cousin who was Mom's good friend. I am not sure where Dad got work, but he didn't get work at the Caterpillar plant where most of his cousins worked.

In the meantime, in Mississippi, as the new school year began, our Aunt Lorna moved into the house with us. Dad's brother, Lonnie, and his wife, Hattie, took the twins, Mary and Martha into their home during this time. The twins were only four years old. Our oldest brother, Aaron, was still a student at Piney Woods School, in Piney Woods, Mississippi. We five girls and baby brother, Dell, stayed in the house with Aunt Lorna.

She was a schoolteacher, so, every morning, we all got up very early to take a sponge bath and get ready for school. For breakfast, we ate a biscuit with egg and fried meat of some kind. Aunt Lorna led the meal preparations. She made the biscuits in the mornings and cooked our vegetables and meats in the evenings.

By this time Betty was fifteen and I was almost fourteen, so we were a big help to Aunt Lorna. Betty washed and combed our hair for school. I was able to stir up cornbread and bake it. We also helped by bringing in the water and making fires in the stove and the fireplace. We washed dishes and cleaned the house. We gathered, cleaned and washed the vegetables to be cooked. We milked the cows, as needed, and strained the milk before putting it away. We churned the milk and put the butter and buttermilk away in the refrigerator, just as Mom had taught us to do. We had a washing machine so wash day every Saturday was not as difficult as it had been earlier.

Auntie kept us from August until Mom returned home from Illinois in December. We were thrilled to have our mother back home with us. Dad returned home in the spring to begin planting crops for the new year. But he decided not to plant cotton in 1962. We children were thrilled about that. It meant less hard work on us for the summer. More importantly, it meant that Dad would not create the large debt of the prior year and the risks that came with that debt. Our lives were back to normal again in our new house.

Chapter 7

No, Not Another Girl!

I vaguely remember when Mom told Betty and me that she was going to have another baby. Betty had turned twenty and I was approaching nineteen. Both of us had been students at Piney Woods Junior College. Betty graduated from high school and had completed two years of Junior College there. I had completed my freshman year of college. Unlike me, Betty was thrilled about the new baby and thought I should be thrilled as well, but I wasn't. My heart sank because it made no sense to me that Mom would have yet another baby when we had so many unmet needs already.

In August 1966, Mom gave birth to one more girl. This gave her a total of eight daughters. Mom let Betty and me name the new baby. We chose the name "Charlotte" because we learned it from a movie called "Hush, Hush, Sweet Charlotte." I don't remember anything about the movie or if I ever saw it. We just liked the name. Betty delighted in her far more than the other sisters. One could say I had a bad attitude toward Charlotte's birth, but my bad feelings did not last very long. As a baby, Charlotte was very pink and had thick, black, wavy hair. After a few months, the redness was gone, and she began to grow into a very beautiful, plump baby girl. We all adored her, but Betty took to mothering her in a way that gave Mom some needed rest. If Char awoke at night, Betty was up right away to see about her. Charlotte benefitted from the extra attention. With the birth of Charlotte, Mom's childbearing years were over. She had turned forty-two, only four days before Charlotte was born.

Char was not yet two years old when she got the measles and had a very high fever one night. Betty was up with Mom tending her while Mom doctored on her. Betty got the big idea that we should all get up from our sleep and sit with them. I resented her waking me up and wanting us to just sit and watch them tend to Charlotte. Maybe we went back to bed that night after Char fell asleep. Fortunately, she got well, and life returned to normal at home.

Char in 1968, and 1970

Later, when Charlotte was a toddler, an event occurred which our sister Sybil says she will never forget because it was so dreadfully frightening. Sybil remembers that Dad opened the barn gate to let the horses go out to the pasture. The horses bolted, running very fast, straightaway toward Charlotte who was sitting on the ground, playing in the dirt in the yard.

Mom and the older siblings were looking on at a situation that could end Char's life if the horses kept their course. All of them looked on, screaming, but afraid to run toward the horses and in great horror for Charlotte. But her guardian angel was already standing there. He directed the horses away from her as they ran, kicking up dust and gravel in their wake. Everyone rushed to get Char off the ground and into the house. They all needed time to let their heartbeats slowdown to normal while they recovered their wits. Mom's faith must have grown "by a mile" after she recovered from that heart-stopping moment. Charlotte has no memory this event which is good, but her older sisters who witnessed it, remember it all too well. After that, Dad made sure that Char was out of the way before he let out the horses again.

Dad & horses

As soon as Charlotte learned to talk, she talked and expressed her observations very freely. She was quick to tell Mom about things the others had done which she thought were "bad." She gave us many shocks by telling others something one of us had said about them in private never meaning that it should be shared. One such time was when our Pastor came for a visit. Charlotte openly told him that Betty called him "peanut head." We were all embarrassed, but we learned to be careful about what we said in her presence.

Charlotte was the only child who watched TV during the day. She watched with hardly any restrictions. We were never allowed to turn on the TV, but Charlotte not only turned it on, she watched it freely. She logged more TV hours than the rest of us altogether. Mom took classes during those years and was probably too tired to deal with the matter. So, when I was home on the summer breaks, I helped Mom by turning off the TV and tried to teach Char to play the piano.

I was a music major in college and was just learning to play the piano myself. I should have known that my controlling way was bound to make Charlotte resist whatever good I wanted to accomplish. Mom agreed with my attempts, but Char would not cooperate. She would fold her arms and tell me, "You can't make me do it." So, most of my good intentions were lost on her. Charlotte was glad to see me go back to college so she could watch TV without limits.

Barbara and Charlotte at piano

Zeola at Head Start in the 1980's

Chapter 8

From the Assembly Line to the Classroom

$\mathcal{B}$etween the years 1963 and 1965, Mom got a job at the chicken plant in Forest, Mississippi, since Mary and Martha were in school every day. She worked along with two or three other women from our community. Mom rode with the others early in the morning to be at work by six o'clock. They had to clock in upon arrival, then straightaway to work.

Every morning, Mom woke us up when she got up. As the oldest at home, it was my job to go to the kitchen with Mom to begin making breakfast. Mom made the biscuits while I fried the meat, and eggs or cooked grits or oatmeal. Mom fixed herself a biscuit to eat on the way to work and something to eat for lunch too. She had no money to buy food in the plant cafeteria. So, she ate whatever she had time to prepare before leaving home. We ate breakfast after she left.

Work on the assembly line was very hard on Mom. She wore metal gloves to protect her from cutting her hands. She noted that the smell was hard to stomach early in the mornings. The work she did while standing was difficult. However, it was made more difficult under an oppressive line supervisor. Fortunately, as God would have it, Mom didn't get to stay much longer than a year before she was fired. The other women continued on at the plant, but Zeola was very happy to stay at home. She was relieved that her mornings didn't have to start so early and that she could take better care of her twins who were seven or eight by that time.

Before the end of 1967, news was rumored that our community was going to get a head start Program. When meetings were held, Mom and Dad went to them. They learned that Mom could apply to work as a teacher and that she would be trained to teach the children. Mom was excited about the prospect. By God's grace, Mom was hired to teach and that began a new career for her.

She took to the role of teacher with great zeal. She had already proven her competence when she kept seventeen children in a six-room house without losing her mind under the stress of it.

From the Assembly Line to the Classroom

 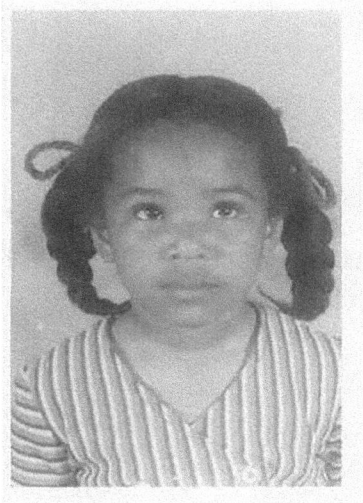

Zeola and Charlotte in Head Start, 1970

Over the next eighteen years, Zeola grew in her skills and knowledge of children and teaching and never lost her love of working with children. She was given the pet name of "Aunt Zee" by the children, and the adults called her Aunt Zee as well. The training was required as long as she worked for Head Start. She had to take all of the courses provided by the Head Start Program. The various courses took her to Holmes Junior College, Jackson State College, Tugaloo College, William Carey Junior College and to the University of Southern Mississippi. In addition to being a devoted teacher, Zeola was a great student. Her grades reflected her scholarship. To her honor, she succeeded on all of the competencies that were required for the Child Development Associate Certificate. She was awarded the CDA in 1986; the first of her peers to earn that honor.

CHAPTER 9

ZEOLA BEGAN WRITING NEWSPAPER COLUMN

*I*n January 1971, a year after the Mississippi public schools were integrated, discussions came up about the need to make some changes in the way The Smith County Reformer covered the local news. The staff of The Smith County Reformer began to look at their weekly publications and realized that they only reported news articles about the local white citizens and communities, so they made the decision to ask the black citizens to write news articles about their communities and offered to publish these weekly as well.

Zeola was asked to write a weekly column for the Reformer providing news from the Mt. Nebo Community. At the time, Zeola had a seven-year-old child in elementary school and twins who were making a change from high school to junior college. She was teaching fulltime in the Head Start Program which meant preparing lesson plans and teaching all week. In addition, she was taking required courses to be trained and certified for the job of teacher which involved travelling out of town for trainings while keeping up with her own assignments and studying new content. Somehow, in spite of her very busy schedule, Zeola accepted the task of writing the weekly column.

Mt. Nebo
by Mrs. Zeola Norris

And this is the confidence that we have in Him: that, if we ask anything according to His will, He heareth us. 1 John 5:14.

Our sincere sympathy to the Lofton families of Pulaski and Chicago, IL in the passing of their loved ones, Mr. Moses Lofton and Mr. L.C. Lofton, brothers who passed away. We pray for you in your hours of bereavement.

We pray this week for Mr. Percy Norris who is in the Veteran's Hospital in Jackson with a hernia.

Happy birthday to Dextris Barnett who celebrated his birthday on April 13th.

r. and Mrs. S.W. ...nilton and Mr. and ...J.H. Jones and fami-...y of Lena, MS visited Mr. and Mrs. Joseph Campbell this week. Mr. and Mrs. William Smith visited them last week.

Ms. Mary Ann Dixon, and Mrs. Ruby Gaye Coleman of Jackson and Mrs.

Columnist Profile

Mrs. Zeola Norris

Her first column was published in the January 3, 1973, Smith County Reformer. Zeola's weekly column reflected the same general concerns of the common people, no matter where they live. Her column included news about community members who were sick, shut-in, hospitalized, or suffering in some other way. Her column also shared good news reports about new babies born, or children who returned to visit their families, birthdays, and various local celebrations. Zeola was diligent to check on different individuals and stories before she wrote the week's news. If she missed seeing someone at church or in person to ask about their families, she made calls on Sunday afternoons or evenings to find out about these members.

She wrote her column every week without many failures. Every week, the news was handwritten on a yellow legal pad and dropped off to the newspaper office on Main Street in Raleigh. Whenever she had a setback, such as being ill or hospitalized which kept her from writing her column, she had her daughter, Brenda, to write it for her. What began in 1973, continued for thirty-eight years, ending sometime in 2011.

Tragedy Broke the Family Circle

In 1973, Zeola's son, Aaron, returned to Mississippi after serving in the army for three terms. He stayed at home a very short time, but it gave his mother great pleasure for the time he was there. His oldest sister, Betty, was living with our parents at the time with her newborn son. She recalls how much pleasure Aaron took in her son and how helpful he was to her while he was there. His cousin, Patricia remembers him staying with her mother awhile and Aaron's enthusiasm for gardening. She was thrilled that he delighted to weed the garden; work that she loathed. His stay with them was a sweet pleasure for them both.

Aaron turned 31on January 1,1974. In the same month that he marked the 31st birthday, Aaron was killed in a tragic accident between Forest and the family home in Raleigh, Mississippi. He had fallen asleep while driving on Saturday afternoon January 26, 1974. He ran off the road and into a tree. The family was devastated to learn of his sudden death. He was already dead when the ambulance picked him up. This was a great sorrow for Zeola; perhaps it was the greatest sorrow she had known at the time.

Aaron in Army Uniform

*This is
the article
Mom wrote
after her
Son's death.*

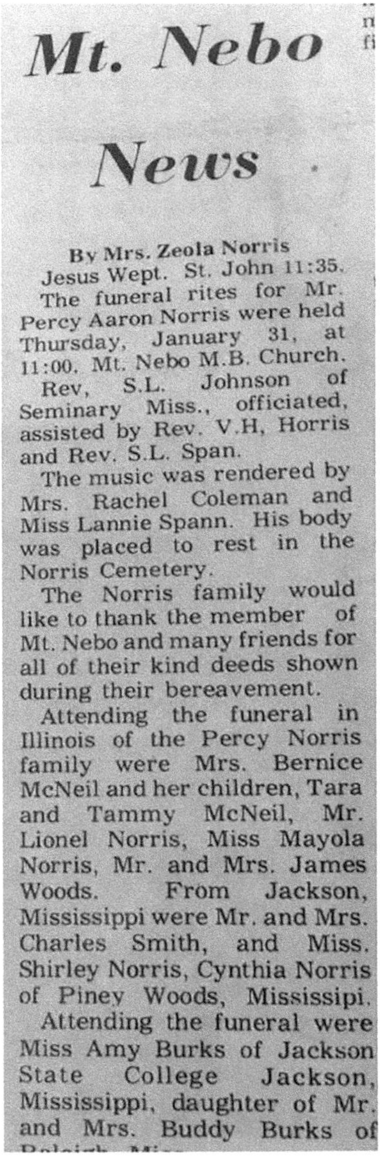

Mt. Nebo

News

By Mrs. Zeola Norris

Jesus Wept. St. John 11:35.

The funeral rites for Mr. Percy Aaron Norris were held Thursday, January 31, at 11:00. Mt. Nebo M.B. Church. Rev, S.L. Johnson of Seminary Miss., officiated, assisted by Rev. V.H, Horris and Rev. S.L. Span.

The music was rendered by Mrs. Rachel Coleman and Miss Lannie Spann. His body was placed to rest in the Norris Cemetery.

The Norris family would like to thank the member of Mt. Nebo and many friends for all of their kind deeds shown during their bereavement.

Attending the funeral in Illinois of the Percy Norris family were Mrs. Bernice McNeil and her children, Tara and Tammy McNeil, Mr. Lionel Norris, Miss Mayola Norris, Mr. and Mrs. James Woods. From Jackson, Mississippi were Mr. and Mrs. Charles Smith, and Miss. Shirley Norris, Cynthia Norris of Piney Woods, Mississipi.

Attending the funeral were Miss Amy Burks of Jackson State College Jackson, Mississippi, daughter of Mr. and Mrs. Buddy Burks of

Thirty-two years later, Zeola faced a second great sorrow with the death of her fourth daughter, Brenda. In May 2001, Brenda was diagnosed with cancer. She had a surgery at the time over that Memorial holiday and after three weeks, she went home and began oral chemotherapy. She lived five years after surgery and treatments, but finally died in May 2006 at the age of 54. Truly, this was another great sorrow in the life of Zeola and her family.

Brenda, January, 2006 four months before her death

In elementary school, Brenda became known to her teachers quickly. Some of them used her to help with many things in the classroom. She was trusted to go to the office to take something or to bring something back to them. We were astounded to learn that her peers elected her to be their homecoming queen. She wore the crown and rode the "Queen's float" in the homecoming parade in her senior year of high school. She was the only daughter who was honored in this way. In the early 1980s, when computers were just coming into use at home, Faye bought a computer and learned how to use it. She was the first person I knew who owned a computer. She then went on to get a position teaching students how to use the computer in her school. Later, when cell phones emerged, she was among the first in our town to own one. She was way ahead of her sisters and her peers in her use of the latest technology.

CHAPTER 10

ZEOLA'S TRAVELS

*D*uring the last ten years of work at Head Start, Brenda arranged for a few road trips for Mom to travel to some places. They went a few times to the Moncrief-Logan Family Reunion in Missouri, Illinois, and Florida. She took Mom on a car trip to Maryland. She met her baby brother in Las Vegas, NV and other brothers in Florida a few times. She took one train trip alone to Maryland, and a trip by air to MD with daughter, Charlotte. On her first airplane trip, Mom wrote a journal entry on each day of that trip. We found the little spiral notebook I gave her earlier. Below are the notes she wrote while on the first visit to Maryland. She wrote the following notes.

Wednesday, August 17, 1988

Miss Charlotte F. Norris and Zeola L. Norris left Jackson, Mississippi Airport. Got on the plane approximately 11:00 a.m. Arrived Nashville, TN airport at 1:20 p.m. Left at 2:30 and reached Philadelphia, PA about 4:30 p.m.

We ate dinner at the Dutch Kitchen in Wilmington, DE. We reached home in Maryland around 11:30 p.m. or later that night.

Thursday, August 18,1988 We went and visited Mrs. Robins in Snow ***Hill, MD.***

Friday, 8-19-88 Barbara, Char and I went shopping at the Mall there in Salisbury, MD We bought a few things then went back home ***and rested.***

Saturday, 8-20-88 We went and visited the Harris family: Uncle Richard, Aunt Millie and Judy their only child. Also met Mrs. Leana and Bud Johnson in ***Oxford, PA.***

Sunday, 8-21-88 We went to church and had seafood dinner at Seafood World. Then went to the Flea Market in ***Laurel, MD.***

Monday, 8-22-88 Charlotte and all of us went to the National Aquarium in ***Baltimore, MD***

Tuesday, 8-23-88 We rested from our long day at ***the aquarium.***

Wednesday, 8-24-88 We went on a cruise down the Wicomico River, then came back and drove to Ocean City, MD. We enjoyed looking at the Atlantic Ocean, and met Rakesh's friends, the Sharma's. Very nice people. Dr. Sharma and wife, warm and lovely, friendly also. We went to the mall in Ocean City and picked up a few ***things there.***

On Wednesday night, Barbara's friends, Sarah, Dorothy and Dorothy's sister who lives in Baltimore visited us. Sarah and Dorothy are both teacher friends of Barbara. They were warm and friendly.

Thursday 8-25-88 We rested and packed that morning and waited for Dorothy and Sarah to come say goodbye. That evening we visited the Boyd family; Eddie, Rosalyn, and children-Faith, Anna and son Theo. Rosalyn cooked a good dinner which included southern fried chicken with gravy and rice. We ate heartily and enjoyed the evening ***with them.***

Friday, 8-26-88 We left Salisbury early, little after 6:00 a.m. Barbara wanted us to see Longwood Gardens before going on to the Philadelphia airport. Charlotte didn't want to go there but enjoyed the visit very much. Then we got on the plane to Nashville, TN by noon. We arrived there safely, then got on the plane for Jackson, MS. We arrived there by 3:45 p.m. We were 15 minutes early. Mary wasn't there, so we waited a little after 4:00 p.m. Then we left for home and arrived in Raleigh about 5:05 p.m. This ended a very nice vacation ***to Maryland.***

April, 1990 Mom travelled by train to be with me for the birth of our baby. She enjoyed the trip by train because she had her own sleeper car and said the people were very nice to her. When Ravi turned four years, Faye arranged for Mom and her family to come by car to Maryland and this turned out to be her very last visit to see us. She saw the foundation of our new house under construction but didn't get to see the house except in pictures.

In the last years of Mom's life, she enjoyed memorizing poems and scriptures. During the time she was recovering from the knee surgery, I went home to visit her. One day she astounded Betty and me when she recited from memory the whole chapter of John 15. Betty recalls that she loved to recite Psalm 100 and/or Psalm 150 on many of their singing occasions.

Betty had many chances to hear her recite verses of scripture and poems. Below is a twelve-stanza poem she memorized and shared on some of their singing events. It was a great delight to hear Mom recite poems and verses.

HEAVEN'S GROCERY STORE

I was walking down life's highway a
long time ago.

One day I saw a sign that read, "HEAVEN'S
GROCERY STORE"
As I got a little closer the door came open
wide And when I came to myself
I was standing inside.

I saw a host of ANGELS. They were standing
everywhere.
One handed me a basket and said, "My Child
shop with care".

Everything a Christian needed was in that grocery store.
And all you couldn't carry,
you could come back the next day for more.

First, I got some PATIENCE: LOVE was in
the same row.
Further down was UNDERSTANDING: You
need that everywhere you go.

I got a box or two of WISDOM, a bag or
two of FAITH.

I just couldn't miss the HOLY GHOST, For it
was all over the place.

I stopped to get some STRENGTH and
COURAGE To help me run this race.
By then my basket was getting full, But I

remembered I needed some GRACE.
I didn't forget SALVATION, For
SALVATION was free,

So I tried to get enough of that To save both
You and Me.
Then I started up to the counter To pay my
grocery bill,
For I thought I had everything To do the
MASTER'S Will.

As I went up the aisle, I saw PRAYER: And I
just had to put that in,
For I knew when I stepped outside, I would
run into Sin.

PEACE AND JOY were plenty They were last
on the shelf.

SONG and PRAISE were hanging near, So I
just helped myself.

Then I said to the angel,
"Now, how much do I owe?" He
smiled and said,
"Just take them everywhere you go."

Again, I smiled and said,
"How much do I really owe?" He smiled
again and said,
"MY CHILD, JESUS PAID YOUR BILL A
LONG, LONG TIME AGO."

Author Unknown

Strong Family Ties

Zeola learned not to hold onto the world tightly or strive for its riches. She had none of the world's riches, but she treasured the people in her life, especially her parents and siblings, who included eight brothers and five sisters. She learned to be content with what she had and to respect and honor her family and friends. Sometimes when we criticized her brothers or Aunt Alla, she made us hush. She would say to us, "if you want to talk about somebody, talk about your own brothers and sisters."

Throughout her life, as long as her health allowed, she got up early every morning to cook breakfast for her husband and family. And even though she was never appreciated by the men that she served like a true servant, she was always faithful to her marriage vows and to her family. She made the holidays fun and cooked many treats for us to enjoy.

For a period in the 1970's, Zeola had another burden added to her already busy household. JW brought his brother, Tood, to stay with them on weekends. Uncle Tood was paralyzed from a stroke which left him in a wheelchair. Somehow, Zeola managed to stay afloat while keeping up with the demands of work, family and home.

A Vibrant Faith

Our Mother was a very special woman of strong faith and devotion to God. She never told us how she came to faith. But she lived out a vibrant faith before us. Her life was full of spiritual growth and commitment to the word of God. She believed God's word and she read it daily as long as she could. She knew Him personally and intimately. During her childrearing years, she began to read her Bible which was the foundation of her faith. If her light was on early in the morning or late in the night, we knew she was reading her Bible or her daily home readings along with the scriptures.

Many mornings, in her last years, we found her asleep with the Bible open because she had dropped off to sleep while reading. During the last years of her life, she read daily from her very worn Bible. She kept some books on her bed as she got older and found herself less able to take them off the shelf or put them back on it.

Zeola was the central person in the family. She showed us how to love and to forgive others, even when the offender didn't ask to be forgiven. I have come to know that she did not empower herself to forgive. She did that hard thing that Jesus commands us to do as He gave her the power to do so. What a faithful woman! Mom exemplified the spirit of the Proverbs 31woman where Verses 29, 30 and 31 conclude:

"Many daughters have done well, but you exceed them all. Charm is deceitful and beauty is passing, but a woman who fears the Lord, she shall be praised. Give her of the fruit of her hands, and let her own works praise her in the gates." NKJV.

Health and Physical Challenges

Although Mom's life was filled with many trials and afflictions, it was also filled with victories over many of them. During her Head Start years, Mom fell on the job. One event involved an accident she had in the classroom which landed her in the hospital and on her back for two weeks. After returning home, her boss refused to report it. A second fall on the job happened as she got off the bus to assist a child across the road. Suddenly, a dog ran out to the bus and knocked her down. This fall was not thought to be serious because nothing appeared to be broken. So medical help was not sought and caused her to go without adequate medical attention at the time. She eventually became crippled in one knee as a result. After some years, she finally got the knee surgery but was left with much pain in her back and knees.

In spite of the knee replacement, she walked with a limp and sometimes the pain kept her in bed in her later years. Because of the pain, she fought depression at different times and took medication to control it for the remainder of her life. In spite of these challenges, Zeola kept striving to do her daily chores of cooking, cleaning and caring for her family, who at the time consisted of only her husband and son. Instead of growing bitter with the trials, she chose to be optimistic and to strive for victory over them. She pressed on most of the time in spite of how she was feeling when she got up.

In the week following her 80th Birthday celebration, Mom fell at home while her sister, (Sugar) Aunt Judie was visiting her. She fell in such a way that her head hit the baseboard and cut a gash that was followed by gushes of blood. She managed to ask for Dell who was providentially just outside the house. Aunt Judie was able to go get him to come inside to help Mom off the floor. Then she had Dell to call Brenda who was able to come to the house after she called for emergency transport. Fortunately for Mom, the EMT team had been on a trip near the community and came very quickly to Mom's aid. She was taken to the Lackey Memorial Hospital in Forest, MS as soon as they got her head bandaged and ready for transport. As they went, they gave emergency help to stop the blood flow.

However, Betty was told by a team member that Mom's blood was dripping so much that it made a pool on the floor as they went. So, he urged the driver to speed up because Mom was losing blood too fast. Fortunately, Betty was able to meet the ambulance at the hospital and provide the information that was needed to do emergency care. Below is a copy of the note, Mom wrote about the fall once she returned home a few days later. Praise the Lord for his providential care of our dear Mother.

My sister Sugar was inside with Me. August 26, 2004 about 3:45 P.M. or 4:00 PM Zeola used Men bathroom, stubbed my left Right right foot, causing me to fall fast and hard, about a foot from the floor, tearing my head 4in. it took 20 Clamps to close the wound. I'm alive Thank God!!!

Mom's Handwritten Note

She wrote many notes of things she wanted to remember. She exchanged a daily soap opera in her years after working fulltime, for the joy of reading her Bible, Sunday School studies and doing word searches and other Bible puzzles whenever I brought them to her.

CHAPTER 11

SHE BEAUTIFIED HER WORLD

*I*n the last few years of Mom's life, she kept busy in the summers planting flowers and vegetable gardens.

Dad was always ready to plow up the soil in early spring if the rains didn't prevent him by making the soil so wet that the tractor would get stuck in the mud. If he used a plow with the horses, the mud would stick to the plow and make it nearly impossible to turn the soil over. If more favorable weather prevailed, a fresh crop of vegetables would be planted very early. Under good conditions, Dad and Mom would have new mustard and turnip greens, lettuce, cabbages, radishes, onions, tomatoes, hot peppers and sweet peppers planted and growing by late March to April.

They often had greens ready to gather and eaten by May. By June, they planted summer vegetables such as sweet corn, butterbeans and peas of many varieties, okra, Irish potatoes and sweet potatoes, watermelons, and cantaloupes. The picture of Mom with granddaughter, Jessica, holding big bunches of broccoli are one example from their garden in the summer of 1990. This picture was taken by a Reformer staff member and published in the Smith County Reformer.

Mom and Jessica Holding Broccoli

Dad Plowing

In addition to the vegetable garden, Mom bought and planted a few kinds of trees to grow in the yard at home. The earliest ones I remember were china berry trees which grew well, but their roots grew out of the ground making big humps around them. This made it difficult to sit in a chair under them. She liked this tree because it didn't attract worms and they made a beautiful green shade tree in the summer. She also bought a snowball shrub for the flowerbed of her son.

American hollies, a silver maple and Bradford pear trees were planted in the yard, but not all grow equally well in the soil near the house. She also cultivated a few fruit trees: plum, peach and apple trees.

The soil was not very conducive for them either or maybe they needed to be pollinated. As a result, the trees never produced any fruit to speak of. Sometimes, we saw little plums or peaches, but they never grew into mature fruit that we could enjoy. A few years after we settled into the new house, Mom transplanted a pecan tree from her mother's yard. For many years it grew very beautifully. She knew enough about this tree to plant it away from the house because in the fall, worms made their nests in it though it never produced any pecans. Perhaps it needed to be pollinated as well. It did grow into a very large, beautiful tree.

One memory I have of Aaron, my oldest brother, happened when he was home one Christmas and took us to look for a Xmas tree. We didn't have much luck finding a nice cedar tree for our Xmas decorations, but we found a beautiful, healthy magnolia growing nearby. So we dug it up and took it home, dug a hole in the yard and planted it. We still have it in the yard today. It gives us shade for parking in the hot summers and we enjoy its fragrance when the flowers bloom.

Crinum Lily

Most of all, Zeola loved flowers and cultivated many beautiful ones, in my childhood such as zinnias, roses, petunias, and verbenas. She had a beautiful white blooming Crinum lily which Mom prized about fifty years. It was in a good place because it produced many beautiful flowers every summer and came back every spring. She also planted a small, pink spider lily which continues to come back in the spring every year. She invested money to fill the planter with beautiful azaleas, and later on she invested to create a rose garden. It took some effort to cultivate roses because they didn't grow well in some of the places she planted them. Sometimes the summer heat and insects destroyed them even if they grew well where she planted them.

Another little habit Mom began to keep was to buy corn to feed the birds in the winter. She started doing that in the last few years of her life. She enjoyed getting some corn in a bucket and carrying it on her walker to the back yard to throw it out to the birds. She delighted to see the blue jays fight each other for it. Sometimes it was mostly big crows and blackbirds. Other times she would see wrens and sparrows, cardinals or red wing blackbirds, and a pair of mourning doves. These were small pleasures that gave Mom joy in simple, country living.

Zeola with Red Amaryllises

A few years ago, Mom invested in beautiful, red amaryllis bulbs which she bought and planted in the fall and waited for their spring flowers. Again, she selected a place near the side of the road which had too much red clay and gravel. It proved to be a poor place for them. The soil did not support their growth. After her death, Sybil and I moved them to the yard to preserve them, but fire ants threatened to destroy them in the new location. So, the following spring, Martha moved them from the yard and planted them in the planter. The amaryllises grew and bloomed beautifully in the planter for two springs. Last summer, they were taken out of the planter and put out in the field away from the house. Now, that reminder of mother's beautiful flowers is no longer there to treasure and enjoy anymore. My hope is that we will cultivate memories of our mother by preserving the flowers she planted and enjoying their beauty whenever we are there. It is a part of her legacy that we can treasure as long as the flowers live.

CHAPTER 12

MOM'S LAST
TWO YEARS

The last two years of Mom's life were fraught with difficulty. January 17, 2011, began with a head-on collision in which Dad and Dell our brother were both injured. Dad's pickup truck was totaled by it. An approaching vehicle going too fast on a narrow road crashed into them and neither of them were able to escape. Both had to be pulled from the truck and carried to the hospital. Even though they were admitted to the hospital, both insisted on going home against the doctor's advice. Mom and my dear sisters endured their foolishness and tried to help them. Dad had to be carried by ambulance the next day when he was in such great pain at home that could not be relieved.

A month later, Mom began to face her own medical challenges: an oozing sore on the leg which refused to heal in spite of medication and therapy. And a blood clot, along with other medical issues, landed her in the hospital on more than one occasion. Through all of these challenges, her daughters were with her, making sure that she kept her appointments, especially when she was most determined to skip them; making sure someone was there with her during her various hospital stays, and making sure that someone was there to see her safely home again when she was discharged. Through it all, the Lord kept Mom and her daughters, especially Betty, our servant sister, through what was a very long trial. At home, our dear sister, Gloria, faithfully cared for Dad and Dell by cooking their food, giving Dad his medicines and keeping his doctor appointments as well. She managed the care of the family home while caring for her home and her own doctor appointments.

Mom entered the hospital for the last time on October 30, 2012. She stayed in Lackey Memorial Hospital in Forest, Mississippi, for one week before being moved to CMMC Hospital in Jackson, Mississippi. Upon arrival there, she was diagnosed with kidney failure and was said to have less than 10% of kidney function. Later that same day, she began to struggle to breathe. And the following day her CT scan showed flat lines. A quick decision was made to put her on a respirator which was done two days later.

We soon began to realize that our dear Mother was going to be in the hospital a long time. As it turned out, she spent the last 200 days of her life in three different hospitals. During that time, Mom was encouraged by Elias Medeiros who came to share the word of God as she lay there on the bed unable to speak or stand. One small joy we gave Mom in the hospital was to let her hear some of her favorite songs on YouTube. Her joy was full whenever she heard these songs. Music played such a large role in her experience and had enriched her life. As long as she could, she sang along with the Clara Ward Singers "I'm Packing Up Getting Ready to Go" and the Angelic Gospel singers "Touch Me Lord Jesus."

On the Saturday night before Mother's Day, 2013, God gave me a vision of my sweet Mother which I will always cherish.

I saw Mom in a beautiful gown lying on her bed and her face was radiant. She smiled her beautiful smile and her countenance glowed. She had no hospital garb, nor any cords attached to her hands or her body.

One week later, on Saturday night after ten o'clock, May 18, 2013, Mom died. Her daughters Sybil and Martha had the honor of being with Mom on the last day of her life on earth.

A Woman of Noble Character

Mom Dressed for Anniversary

"Remember your leaders, those who spoke to you the word of God. Consider the outcome of their way of life, and imitate their faith." Hebrews 13: 7 ESV Bible

One morning as I read my devotion for that day, the words in Hebrews 13: 7 spoke clearly to me and helped me to understand why I had undertaken the task of celebrating Zeola's life. The lessons we can learn from Zeola's life cannot all be recounted. The life lessons Zeola exemplified don't seem doable in today's environment. She disciplined and corrected her children because the Bible said to teach children while they are young: "Train up a child while he is young and when he is old, he will not depart from it." Proverbs 22:6 She left a legacy of strong commitments: to God, to family, to neighbors, to church, and to community.

Even though her life has ended, Zeola's conduct can provide valuable life lessons for her children and for all who would consider her way of life and imitate her faith. It is important that we, Zeola's posterity, remember the Godly character that was forged on her journey through life's trials and sorrows. More importantly, we can examine the pattern and outcome of her life as a follower of Christ and strive to imitate her faith and character.

Family Pictures

Mom and Dad, December 1979

Barbara on wedding day, December 1979

Barbara with sisters, December 1979

Mom, Dad, sisters and brother, August 2004

Mom, and daughter with sisters, August 2004

Mom, Dad and Grandchildren, August 2004

Mary, Nonye and Fidel

Nonye& William 5/27/17

Jaylan, Ravi, and Khilan 5/27/17

Barbara and son Ravi 5/27/17

Grand and Great grandchildren 12/25/2019

Grandchildren 12/25/19

Barbara Norris Arya

Keith and Teela 2/14/21

Kevin and Melanie 2/19/2022

Ravi and Sarah 11/5/22

Ravi and Sarah 11/5/22

Ravi and Sarah 11/6/22

Ravi and Sarah 11/6/22

Rakesh, Barbara, Ravi and Sarah 11/6/22

Rakesh and Barbara 11/6/22

JOHN WILEY and ZEOLA NORRIS FAMILY: 4 GENERATIONS

1st. Generation	JW & Zeola	
2nd Generation	3rd Generation	4th Generation
1. Aaron & Rose (S)	Christopher & Carla (S)	Leah & Layla
2. Bettye & Jimmy (S)	Perez & Sheila (S)	Alexus
	Meshan & Dorsett (S)	Jaylon & Jace
3. Barbara & Rakesh (S)	Ravi & Sarah (S)	
4. Gloria & Charles (S)	Kristy	
	Misty	
	Charla & Marla (twins)	
5. Brenda & Austin (S)	Cory Dujuan	
Brenda & Edward (S)	Jessica Faye	Jayla
6. Sybil & Al (S)	Stephanie & Aaron (S)	Ariana & Caleb
	Melanie & Kevin (S)	
	Keith & Teela (S)	Brylee & Baylor
7. James Cordell		
8. Mary & Fidel (S)	Emeka & Erica (S)	Derica & Moriah
		Josiah & Zeniah
	Chika	Michael & Malia
	Nonye & William (S)	
9. Martha & Rick	Steven	Cameron & Caleb
	Carol	
10. Charlotte & Joseph (S)	Monica	
	Patrice	

CHAPTER 13

ZEOLA'S LEGACY
FROM A TO Z

$\mathscr{S}$ummarizing the legacy Mom left us has been my pleasure. I have used the letters of the alphabet to remember some of her teachings and morals she treasured and applied to us. Some of them are scriptures she quoted. Others are from songs she sang or proverbs she knew and used. Her intellectual strength was not a matter of pride, but a skill she used to understand and apply God's word. A few of the letters are the names of her family members whom she loved. She left a rich legacy for us to cherish and to share with our children and grandchildren: Mom's posterity.

- **A. Aaron**- the name given to her first son and the name of one of her brothers. "**Ask** and it will be given, seek and you will find, knock and it will be opened..." Matthew 7:7
- **B. Bible** is the book which Mom cherished. She was blessed by the birth of five girls in sequence. **Betty, Barbara and Brenda** are her three "Bees."

C. **Charlotte** is the last daughter of eight and the last of ten children. Matthew 11:28-30 Jesus said, "Come to me all you who labor and are heavy laden, and I will give you rest."

D. **"Draw** near to God and He will draw near to you." James 4:8 **Dell** is the pet name of our brother, **James**.

E. **"Every** good gift and every perfect gift is from above, and comes down from the Father of lights, with whom there is no variation or shadow of turning." James 1:17

F. **"Faith** is the substance of things hoped for, the evidence of things not seen." Hebrews 12:1 **Faye** was the pet name of our sister, **Brenda**.

G. **Gloria** is the third daughter of Zeola. **"Glory to the Newborn King"** was a favorite song that Mom taught us to sing.

H. HOPE. Mom had the **Hope of HEAVEN** when this life would end. **"Rejoice in Hope, be patient in tribulation, be persistent in prayer."** Romans 12:12.

I. For with God nothing will be IMPOSSIBLE. Luke 1:37

J. **JESUS,** is the Savior that Mom put her trust in. **J** is also for **John**, the name of her husband, and **James** the second son in Mom's legacy.

K. **KEEP** your eyes on **KING Jesus,** Mom told us.

L. **"LOVE** one another, as I have loved you." John 15:12 Mom showed love in her role of daughter, sister, wife, mother, and friend.

M. **Mary** and **Martha** are the twins of Mom's legacy.

N. "For with God **Nothing** shall be impossible. Luke 1:37

O. "Children, **Obey your parents** in the Lord, for this is right." Ephesians 6:1 This is one of the many scriptures Mom taught us.

P. **"Pray Continually."** 1 Thessalonians 5:17 Mom taught us to **Pray**. She believed in the **power of prayer.**

Q. "Beloved brethren, let every man be **QUICK** to hear, slow to speak, and slow to get angry. "James 1:19 "Do not **Quench** the spirit." 1Thessalonians 5:19

R. **"Remember** your creator in the days of your youth." Ecclesiastes 12:1 **"Repay** no one evil for evil. Have regard for good things in the sight of all men." Romans 12:17

S. "I will **SING** to the Lord as long as I live; I will sing praise to my God while I have my being." Psalm# 104:33 Mom left a legacy of singing. She loved to sing and was always ready to sing praises to God. **Sybil** is the fifth of the five girls in sequence.

T. **"Trust** in the Lord with all your heart, and do not lean on your own understanding." Proverbs 3:5

U. "Strive to keep the **Unity** of the spirit in the bond of peace." Ephesians 4:3 Mom cried many tears over the breakup of Mt Nebo church. She wanted to see it united as one body again, but she did not live to see it. May we pray and wait for God to redeem it.

V. **"Vengeance** is mine, I will repay says the Lord." Romans 12:19

W. "Take heed, **Watch** and pray; for you do not know what hour your Lord is coming." Matthew 24: 42 **"Walk** by faith; not by sight." 2 Corinthians 5:7

Y. **"Take my Yoke** upon you and learn from me, for I am meek and lowly in heart." Matthew 11:29

Z. **Zeola** had a **zeal** to know God. She searched the scriptures to know Him. Acts 17:11

www.ingramcontent.com/pod-product-compliance
Lightning Source LLC
Chambersburg PA
CBHW051639120626
46551CB00014B/2133